Dominate your market
with Twitter

Dominate your market with Twitter

Tweet your way to business success

Jo

infinite**ideas**

CAREFUL NOW

There are both good and bad sources of information available on the Internet, in the telephone directory, and advertised on bad photocopies for 20p a week in the local newsagents. The Internet especially is a constantly changing phenomenon and therefore good (and bad) sites are forever popping up and dropping off. Web addresses change, so if a link doesn't work, be sure to use Google (or your preferred search engine) to try and find its new home, or a similar service offered by another firm or individual. Likewise, you should have an up-to-date virus checker installed before you visit new sites and download anything whatsoever and you should be aware that new applications may squabble and bicker over who's the daddy – they might not work because of what else you have installed on your machine. We're very sorry about all this and wish it was a better world, but it's the only one we have. We believe in taking it on the chin like grown ups and expect you to do the same. We love you dearly but if it all goes kumquat shaped then you're on your own; we take no liability. See it as an adventure...

Copyright © Jon Smith and José Llinares, 2009

The right of Jon Smith and José Llinares to be identified as the authors of this book has been asserted in accordance with the Copyright, Designs and Patents Act 1988.

First published in 2009 by
The Infinite Ideas Limited
36 St Giles
Oxford, OX1 3LD
United Kingdom
www.infideas.com

A CIP catalogue record for this book is available from the British Library

ISBN 978–1–906821–16–6

Brand and product names are trademarks or registered trademarks of their respective owners.

Cover designed by Cylinder
Typeset by Baseline Arts Ltd, Oxford
Printed and bound by TJ International, Cornwall

Contents

Introduction

Social networking is this year's black. It will probably be next year's black too. Leading the charge and this 'fashion revolution' is Twitter. The idea that an application which allows users to write text-based posts of up to 140 characters could be so popular (at the time of writing there are some 8 million users of Twitter worldwide) boggles the mind – and yet it *is* popular and continues to grow. Twitter has recently confirmed a successful third round of funding netting them a further $35 million to spend on product development…

Why the fuss? Why does Twitter need a book? Well, like it or loathe it, there's something about Twitter that works. Individuals are using it to communicate with each other for fun (and in some extreme cases to report they've been arrested in hostile countries or got lost on a mountain) and companies are using it to successfully market themselves and, crucially, to make money. Twitter can be grouped as part of the general social marketing milieu, but it is its own beast, quite separate from the large social networking web sites. It has its own rules, its own potential and therefore needs to be embraced by an individual or a corporation whenever you are planning to communicate via the internet.

This book is intended for individuals, bloggers, web site owners, marketing managers, project managers and anyone interested in promoting themselves, their group or their business effectively. It is for the non-techie who wants to be involved. It will show you how to research, prepare and run your own

Twitter social marketing campaign and will also give you the tools and the confidence to be able to explain to other team members, clients and anyone else you care to talk to, about what Twitter is doing for you, and what it can do for them.

There is no official guide to how you can make Twitter work better for you, your group or organisation, or your business, but we trust you will find this 'unofficial' guide to be clear, concise and effective. We've tested these techniques on a number of accounts, both high profile and the more obscure; we assure you they work, and they work well. Ready to get started? Then let us take your hand (metaphorically speaking, of course!) and let's Tweet until we can tweet no more....

Chapter one
Twitter – what's it all about?

In the beginning....

Our professional online marketing careers began in 1998 when the Internet as a medium for exchanging information was already established, (well, certainly among techies and academics). The whole concept of electronic communication to and by the masses was still very much in its infancy. Social networking was a phrase that was still to be coined. Fast forward to the present day and we're awash with blogs, email, web sites, applications, widgets, social networking and ever-new ways to distribute and receive

1

information. Twitter is the latest of these 'tools' that will apparently make our lives better, make companies more competitive and profitable and even improve our sex lives. I might be making the last bit up.

So, with all of the noise out there, what makes Twitter special, why will it succeed where others fail and how can I dominate my market using it?

Well, hopefully this book will answer that question and better explain why Twitter is taking the internet world by storm as well as making the print media sit up and take notice; here are just a few recent comments.

"one of the fastest-growing phenomena on the Internet."
The New York Times

"Twitter is on its way to becoming the next killer app."
TIME Magazine

"Suddenly, it seems as though all the world's a-twitter."
Newsweek

What on earth is Twitter anyway?

Twitter is, at first glance, completely mad; tell the world what you are doing in 140 characters or less, and read what the world is doing in 140 characters or less. Simple, yet extremely powerful. Twitter is the 'marmite' of internet applications – it has some hardcore followers who see it as revolutionary and it has its fair share of detractors who just think it's plain stupid. Twitter is ridiculously easy to use, and therein lies its strength – a low barrier to entry and simple raison d'être, yet it has already spawned hundreds of Twitter-based applications, a worldwide following and is used, daily, by millions.

...Err, sorry...What?

OK, a few definitions first. Often commentators refer to online communities and social networks as if they are the same thing. But there are some differences.

A community is based on a strong tie relating to a subject (known as the 'social object') and people gather together around it. Online communities therefore centre on a common subject of interest, and the members of the community discuss, share opinions and socialise. The best examples of online communities are online forums. Online forums are always focused on a specific subject; programming, cooking, films… Once you have registered on an online forum you can access all of the information, take part in discussions and have access (such as the ability to send direct messages) to the other members.

Social networks are based on let's say 'loose ties', they are more people connectors than information depositories. People may join a social network because they have a similar interest to other members, which allows the connection, but the network is broad and allows migration into other areas of interest. Currently, the most popular example of social networking is Facebook. When you first create an account in Facebook it doesn't have any value to you; you need to add friends in order to make that network relevant, to access more information and to begin communicating. Social network ties are broad although the initial 'connector' may be your school, college or place of work. Facebook users use their account to merge all of their different social and sometimes professional circles.

As always definitions are blurred and borders are weak; people with similar interests naturally gather together, and of course within the broad network of Facebook it is possible to create Groups to more closely bond with others who share a common interest ('social object'), or share pictures or videos that will gather like-minded individuals to you… so you see there are differences, but the boundaries of when a community becomes a social network remain hazy.

So, where does Twitter sit? According to Twitter founder Jack Dorsey, Twitter is neither an online community nor a social network, for him Twitter is a new communication tool that cannot be categorised within the existing framework. What Twitter allows is a new way of communicating with others, as we will show. Twitter creates a new communication tempo that converts this application into something perfect for fast, flexible, non-intrusive and portable communications. Saying that, in order to get the most out of Twitter you need to connect with people who are relevant to you, so you have to create your own network and usually that network is related to a subject (music, marketing…). Therefore we can say that Twitter has a little bit of everything; it allows you to communicate in a different way, it allows you to create a network of interesting people and to share and discuss interesting topics with like-minded people.

In the end of course it is how you decide to interact with Twitter that will determine whether it's one thing or another. Maybe you just use it to stay in contact and keep abreast of what your friends and colleagues are doing; or maybe you just want to find the most interesting articles about Search Engine Marketing and discuss them.

Who's responsible for this child of Satan?

Twitter was founded by Evan Williams, Biz Stone, Noah Glass and Jack Dorsey; a group of individuals obsessed with the Web 2.0 revolution, the semantic web and a net run by people and not by companies. These guys didn't think that social networking was now complete because we have Facebook, LinkedIn and MySpace. They created Twitter to continue to unlock even more potential within the social web and to encourage further communication, sharing and learning from one another. Twitter was born inside the blogger world, one area that was already changing the way people communicate between themselves. In fact, Twitter and other similar services are known as microblogging tools; don't worry if you still don't understand what microblogging means... we'll explain both the concept and how you too can microblog throughout this book.

Initial reactions to Twitter, generally, were very derisory. I already have my web site to update, my Facebook profile, LinkedIn, Xing, my blog, etc. There simply aren't enough hours in the day to do all this properly, and still hold down a full-time job! But early adopters set the stage and showed how easy it was to send and receive regular messages through Twitter – it wasn't long before it went viral. According to

Nielsen data, Twitter grew by 422% in 2008 reaching nearly 8 million users and despite being the new boy in class, was outperforming even Facebook in terms of percentage growth. Twitter, due to its ease of use and flexibility has achieved a huge community of users...

Seeing the effect

To see that effect for real, check out local blogs and sites about any Twitter events that are happening in your area. In Barcelona, for example, once a month we have *Cava&Twitts* where Twitter users gather together to drink Cava and talk about Twitter. The emphasis is on the sharing of information; so individuals representing themselves or their business talk about what they've done with Twitter, and what Twitter is doing for them. In the few months since it's been running, membership is growing by about fifty people a week and finding a suitable venue will soon be quite difficult.

If that wasn't enough we also have Twittbarna where users gather together, this time to drink beer and put a face to the people they are talking to via Twitter. This is just in Barcelona… get involved with what's happening in your area and start discovering the exciting world of Twitter … and we will be more than happy if you let us know about events in your region.

Getting started

Twitter is a really simple application. To start you just need to register by creating a user name and you're ready to start sending messages across the worldwide web by writing in a text box using no more than 140 characters 'saying what are you doing'.

Each one of these status updates is affectionately known as a 'Tweet'. Basically, that's pretty much it...

What do I have to do?
Let's start by explaining the Twitter application and its elements.

Twitter is a web-based application; a program that runs and allows you to interact through http protocols, which means that it can be executed through your web browser (Internet Explorer, Mozilla Firefox, Safari or your browser of choice) – the same protocol in fact that your favourite web site or email client (such as Gmail or Hotmail) uses.

You can access Twitter at http://www.twitter.com and register as a user. Of course the site is pretty self-explanatory and the best way to learn is to try, however here's what you will need to bear in mind:

The registration process.

First choose a user name which fits in with how you wish to employ Twitter. If you are using it for personal purposes (i.e. staying in contact with friends) then use your nickname, if you are using it for self-promotional purposes it's better to use your name (first+last name) assuming it's still available and if it is for your company then it kind of makes sense to use your company name! Don't forget you can use underscore and hyphens to give you more options. Remember that a company is made up of individuals: you have to decide whether you want your image to be 'corporate' or whether you want it to be the 'human face', in which case attaching a personality to the Twitter account may assist in gaining trust and transparency; something users love. If your company operates across a number of countries then it's best to have a separate account for each of the territories so that you can communicate to your existing and potential customers in their preferred language. For example, we're promoting a product called Deenero via Twitter. Because we want to tailor our messages (and the language of the messages) to a specific audience, rather than creating a generic Deenero Twitter account, we have @deenerofrance and @deeneroespana, and as we launch new countries, new Twitter accounts will be created.

You have the opportunity to 'see if your friends are on Twitter' – being alone on Twitter simply doesn't work – you need followers to read your Tweets. Otherwise it's like shouting in the middle of the forest. Twitter will ask for your email address and for you to create a password. With your permission, Twitter will scan your email address book and inform you which of your contacts are already using Twitter, in case you don't feel comfortable with this step don't worry, you can skip it.

So now you have some Followers on Twitter, it's equally important to ensure that you are Following others, so that you can read their Tweets. Twitter will try to help you access interesting information and will recommend some popular (but not necessarily relevant) Twitter users like Al Gore or the writer Chuck Palahniuk. Of course you can always edit your list of contacts and add or delete as many users as you want. There are also applications that will allow you to grow your list of people to Follow which will be discussed later.

And the next step… no, that's it! You have joined the Twitter community.

Need a destination on Twitter to get you started? Well, you are very welcome to wander over to our Twitter pages which can be found at:

http://twitter.com/sanseng
(@sanseng)
http://twitter.com/josellinares
(@josellinares)

Your profile

Now you are a full card-carrying member of Twitter you have the opportunity to personalise how you appear to others. Don't worry, Twitter loves to keep things simple, so thankfully you don't have to remember what years you went to school, or when you got your first job, or whether you have any pets – in fact, one of the most important things about Twitter's success is that you are up and running and ready to use Twitter in about thirty seconds. Twitter is not about creating a complex profile, and bamboozling you with lots of 'time-saving' widgets and hardcore functionality... we have enough of that everyday just getting to grips with Windows Vista. Twitter is both simple, and, at the same time incredibly flexible, allowing you to grow with the concept as and when you're ready.

Create your bio

Now that you have registered you can create your bio (in less than 160 characters). Less is more baby! At first this character limit seems, well, limiting – how can I possibly explain to the world what I am and what I want to be in a couple of sentences – but it's this very minimalist approach that is something you will end up loving about Twitter… keeping things simple and getting straight to the point.

Add your web site

To complement your bio you can add the URL of your web site, if you have one. Your personal web site can tell your followers lots about you, so you don't have to repeat it all in your bio – and if you're looking to market your company to users, then they'll be able to click through and read all the information there. Use the bio area to explain what you're using Twitter for – be it promotions, customer relationship management or whatever… and don't worry if you don't have a web site, Twitter can be your page on the web now!

Public or private updates?

Twitter is primarily an open form of communication between users and for that reason Twitter updates are public and therefore seen by anyone who visits your profile page so that they may benefit from the useful information you are posting. If you don't feel comfortable with this public arena, want more 'privacy' or simply want to create a private Twitter network, you can mark your updates as private. This means that in order to see your updates, users will need to ask for permission and you will need to accept their request.

Upload your photo

You can upload a picture, something that we really recommend you do. As you've now realised, there's not a tremendous amount of opportunity to post information about yourself or your company on your

Twitter account, so a picture becomes a key element. It's always nice to put a face to the people we 'talk' with on Twitter, and from a corporate perspective, branding is always key. For personal accounts we recommend a legitimate head and shoulder shot, but if you want to be informal you can always use the picture of your cat. Anything is better than the default Twitter image which reeks of 'I can't be arsed' rather than 'it's cool to be anonymous'.

Use your mobile

It's within your profile that you can elect to use your mobile phone both for posting Tweets and for receiving Tweets all via SMS. Don't worry; this is something you can change later, if you're not sure how 'connected' you want to be.

Personalise your Twitter page

Lastly, you have the opportunity to personalise the design of your Twitter page – for the less adventurous among you, there's a selection of pre-designed templates to choose from, or, if you're not a fan of wearing the same clothes as everyone else, now's your chance to put your stamp on your page. I actually quite like the black template design, so I've stuck with it. For now.

The Followed and Followers...

By far the most important concepts on Twitter; **Following** and **Followers** are the concepts that will determine your relationship with the *Twittersphere*. There are those who wish to read what you post – Followers, and those whose posts you wish to read – Following. Your relationship to both and the equilibrium you create between the two will determine, and be determined by how you interact with Twitter.

Following

The people whom you are Following are the people that you are 'listening' to; friends, family, colleagues or even people or companies you've come across on the web or through Twitter. The people you choose to Follow will be the ones whose mini-image icons will appear on your homepage, the people who you want to focus your attention on – so make sure they're pretty interesting!

Before Following someone on Twitter always ask yourself, 'is that person and the things he or she is writing about relevant to me?' Remember that incoming

Tweets soon add up and you want to make sure that the information is both relevant and interesting.

Every time you decide to Follow a user, that user receives an email notification to alert them about their new Follower. They then have the option to check you out and decide if they would like to Follow you too. The good news is that you can decide to Follow someone at any point and equally you can decide you no longer wish to Follow someone at a later stage…

There's a common misconception that randomly following as many users as possible is the fastest way to get noticed and become popular – in the vain hope that everyone you follow will feel obliged to follow you. This is definitely not the case. If you just truly want to get noticed, following as many people as possible is not the best way. Think about the real world; imagine someone who is constantly giving out their business card to random strangers but is not interested in what you have to say or in your friends. This constant 'look at me' mentality is tiresome and any relationship, be it on or offline, starts with two-way communication. You will follow users because what they say is interesting to you and equally they will only choose to follow you if indeed you are interesting to them. We will look at this again throughout the book to ensure you get the most out of Twitter.

Followers

A Follower is someone who is interested in you, your company, your opinions, your expertise or even your witty retorts. They want to receive your updates or

Tweets. This means that every time you Tweet, your followers will be reading it. A Twitter account without followers is like talking to the wall. So, you're going to have to get yourself some followers!

The first problem is if no one knows who you are, they're unlikely to want to listen to you? How can you make them aware of all the amazing things you have to say? Of course you have the chance to say to your friends and colleagues that you are on Twitter, so they can start Following you and start receiving your Tweets.

Twitter will also help you get started – through the 'Find People' tab you can log in to your web-based email account such as Hotmail, Gmail or Yahoo and add your contacts this way, or you can 'Find on Twitter' by searching by name or nickname. You can invite directly by email or allow Twitter to suggest users to you. If you haven't found someone to invite to be your Follower within half an hour of opening your account you've probably got some offline issues with forging relationships which I'm afraid Twitter won't fix! Lastly of course, assuming you've found an individual or a company that you are interested in learning more about, you can start to Follow other users!

Communicating your Tweets
@Replies for all your Followers

Twitter is for posting Tweets and also to be able to read other's Tweets, but the defining difference that separates it from blogs or even forums is how it encourages conversation. When you notice an interesting Tweet you can reply direct to that user using the @replies function – by clicking on the user name such as @sanseng, you will be able to write (publicly) to that user.

A simple tweak of your account settings will allow you to see any @replies addressed to you on your Twitter homepage (even if you don't follow the user who @replied to you) so you never miss these messages. Replies are easily identifiable because they always have this pattern @user-name [tweet content]. If you wish to reply to their @reply simply click on their user name and Tweet away. @replies are the fastest way to build up friends and followers on Twitter because they clearly show to the recipient and to your other followers that you are addressing other users direct about specific topics, providing information, answers or just your opinion. But to one and all you are quite clearly a communicator – and this is critical to your success on Twitter.

Direct messages for a specific Follower and privacy
Do remember that @replies are visible to all Twitter users. This is deliberate as they usually can add value both to your account and of course to other users. There are of course some Tweets that you don't want the whole world to know about – this might be personal views you wish to share with one other user, or a business decision to take a certain thread 'offline'. Don't worry, you can still use Twitter to communicate privately by sending a Direct Message addressed to a specific user. Simply choose Direct Message, select a user from the drop down, write and send your Tweet. A Direct Message is just that, a private message to a specific user (still limited to 140 characters).

Retweeting

Retweeting is broadcasting something you have picked up from a user you Follow, which you choose to share with those who Follow you. Some Tweets are so interesting, relevant, important, topical or just hilariously funny that you want to spread the word among your followers. This is called a Retweet. Remember to be generous to the user who shared the information with you and to mention your sources and attribute the merit to whom it belongs; that way you will get far more respect than trying to look the best informed guy in town.

There is an etiquette to Retweeting. You should clearly mark that the information is a Retweet, this can be done by starting your Tweet with 'RT', then the source '@user name' and finally the link or information.

Tagging

One of the most important things about providing and storing information is how best to organise it. As web users we're generally getting better at both finding data and marking or tagging data so that it can be found by others. If you've dabbled with Search Engine Optimisation or web design you'll be familiar with the importance of metadata and Header Tags to alert both the search engines and web users where they can find the important information on your web pages. Well Twitter is no different. Often it is the case that the valuable information you require does indeed exist, but you simply can't find it. With millions of Tweets being written every single day, there has to be a system that allows users to find what they want without having to trawl through kilometres of random text – and there is... it's called Tagging.

A Tag is a word you can associate to a piece of information that tries to describe it and therefore allows it to be found.

Tagging is done manually, and to do it, you have to add '#' and the Tag you wish to apply. Once your Tweet is tagged you make the lives of other Twitter users infinitely easier. Now, if I'm looking for more information about Google I can just search for #google and find all the information that users believe is relevant to that subject.

Remember that it's users themselves who create Tags, and therefore there is a huge gulf in accuracy depending on which Tag you are searching for. Remember, it's up to you how you apply Tags, but to make the system work, be as accurate as you can. This

 conciertosbcn

▶ ✓**Following** ─Device updates OFF

Concierto 03-04-2009: HUMAN
ADULT BAND (USA) :: HEMISFERI
DRET (MIEMBROS DE LES AUS,
ZEIDUN I LA ORQUESTA DE LA ..
http://tinyurl.com/cxewvo

cerca de 4 horas ago from twitterfeed

Concierto 03-04-2009: HUMAN ADULT BAND http://tinyurl.com
/ceqora
cerca de 5 horas ago from twitterfeed

Concierto 03-04-2009: GOD WILLING + UNICORN HARD-ON
http://tinyurl.com/dcxk5v
cerca de 6 horas ago from twitterfeed

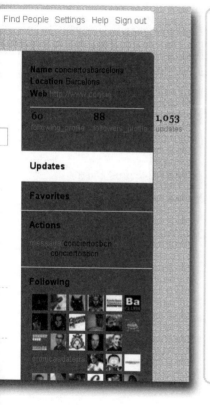

Find People   Settings   Help   Sign out

Name conciertosbarcelona
Location Barcelona
Web http://www.conci...

60   88   1,053
following_profile followers_profile updates

Updates

Favorites

Actions
message conciertosbcn
conciertosbcn

Following

way, other Twitter users and web surfers are more likely to find your Tweet and you.

The profile page

We have been talking about Profile Pages indirectly but probably it needs a little bit more explanation. The Profile Page is a user's home page – from here you are able to see all their updates or Tweets and of

33

course see their basic profile information. Every user gets their own page on Twitter – so if you didn't have a homepage before, you do now. Your Twitter page can be accessed from this address: http://www.twitter.com/user-name (replace user-name with your actual Twitter user name).

❀ The profile information and user name. (All the information you completed when registering your Twitter account).
❀ The number of people the user is Following. And the profile pictures of a selection of those who are being Followed.
❀ The number of people who are Following the user.
❀ The number of Tweets the user has posted – which allows others to see how active the user is on Twitter.

❀ Updates – the user's Tweets listed in chronological order.

❀ Favourites – a summary of the user's favourite Tweets posted by others.

❀ Actions – if you're being Followed by the user then you have the option to block them and if you're not following them, you have the option to Follow them.

❀ RSS – you can elect to have a user's Tweets fed to you through your favourite RSS Reader, so you don't need to log into Twitter, or you can utilise one of the host of Twitter Apps listed later in the book to stay abreast of a user's latest Twitter activity.

Home is where the heart is

Your homepage is your control dashboard, from where you see everything pertaining to you in the

What are you doing?

Latest: @yondri El PR3 ya lo tenías, simplemente hoy se muestra en la toolbar la actualización es sólo visual ;) ¡enhorabuena de todos modos! 18 minutos ago

Home

ascarida e despois de Magnolia, The Omen
5 minutos ago from TwitterFox

the_gman 101 Blogging Tips I've Learned in 2008
http://is.gd/dack
10 minutos ago from web

yondri @josellinares **gracias =)**
11 minutos ago from TweetDeck in reply to josellinares

avinashkaushik Scary/Awesome: "In 5 yrs losing a int

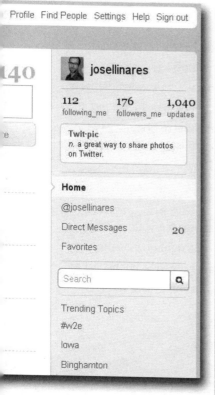

Profile Find People Settings Help Sign out

josellinares

112   176   1,040
following_me followers_me updates

Twit·pic
n. a great way to share photos
on Twitter.

Home

@josellinares

Direct Messages   20

Favorites

Search   🔍

Trending Topics

#w2e

Iowa

Binghamton

Twittersphere. Your homepage gives you a snapshot of all the latest activity on Twitter and easy access to whoever from your network has been Twittering, and what indeed they're Tweeting about. On the top navigation you can also access your Profile Page – this is how other users will see you – your latest updates, your bio, number of followers, etc.

The Twitter search

Recently Twitter has added a search functionality, which borders on the fantastic. This is real-time search baby! Google is great… but sometimes you need, just that, to know things in real-time. Test it for yourself. Include a brand name or obscure word in your Tweet, and then search for it – it's been indexed and is accessible by every Twitter user immediately. Incredible.

Coupled with the instant search is your access to 'Trending topics'. What's hot, right now on the Twittersphere? You always wanted to be the first to know and Twitter trends can be your best friend for that.

Chapter two
The keys to success

What next?

So now you're armed with your new Twitter account, know your way around the dashboard and you're all ready to go. So... What next? I think it's fair to say, on first appearance, Twitter doesn't look like much – I've heard 'it's just another stupid application' and 'this year's Facebook' quite a few times. 'Twitter is too simple and too basic to be of any value or use to me or my business'. But don't judge Twitter on your first impressions, think about SMS: did you think texts were a great idea the first time you realised the feature was available on your mobile? I bet you've sent a fair few since then. Basically, you'll fall in love with Twitter the more you use it and we'll give you a helping hand so you know where to look.

We can't stress enough how important it is just to play with Twitter, get used to its functionality and see what others are using it for. It is then that you realise it's not just for geeks, but a whole new communication channel that's ready and willing to accept your input.

A new communication tempo

Twitter is something between Instant Messaging (IRC, Messenger, Gtalk, etc.) and blogging. It is not instant messaging because your audience doesn't necessarily read Tweets as they're posted in real-time and you don't always read your received Tweets as they are published. Twitter is not blogging because the word limit of 140 characters is a design feature that frustrates efforts to write long diatribes. Twitter is something that sits somewhere in between; a hybrid that merges the synchronous communication provided by Instant Messaging services and asynchronous information provided by blogs.

The world is moving at a faster and faster rate – businesses succeed or fail on their ability to capture, process and provide information to their customers and suppliers. Twitter fills a gap. We are so busy that we don't have time to be talking directly to everyone, whether they are friends or clients – we need to focus on our tasks and move on to the next one. However, our average day, although busy, is full of small spaces of 'free' time that can't be used for productive purposes and Twitter is the perfect medium to allow a two-minute window to be truly productive.

Biz Stone, one of Twitter's founders, says that Twitter offers a new form of human communication and I don't think he's too far off the mark. Twitter opens new ways to communicate. Thanks to Twitter you can access a conversation when you want to, in real-time or retrospectively. Twitter doesn't bother you with annoying alerts to say you've got unread messages or @randomfriend has hurt his toe getting out of bed this morning (unless of course you want it to!). The 140 characters limitation allows you to scan small bite-sized pieces of information, keep informed about what friends and colleagues are up to and, if you want to, add to the lexicon yourself by posting a Tweet.

Conversely if you want real-time, you get it! The immediateness of Twitter has allowed it to grow into a great tool for tracking relevant events. The first news and pictures about the Spanair plane accident that took place in Madrid appeared via Twitter. The US Airways plane ditching in the Hudson was being Tweeted before the press and the photographers could make it over the water in a boat. Israel's attack on Gaza was first reported on Twitter, Stephen Fry got trapped in a lift… Twitter is the new Associated Press and what is more important is that the information comes from the people themselves; the witnesses, the victims, the affected – and not the media agencies or journalists who may wish to censor the information released.

Flexibility

As a consequence of its simplicity, Twitter is really flexible, fitting myriad different purposes. Twitter, if you strip it down, is just a box for posting 140 characters. You can write whatever you want in that box; you can say what you are doing, but you can also send an @reply or a Direct Message to someone. You can use it to remember things or to add valuable information or to share valuable information. Or, you can just tell us that it's pretty sunny outside. You can use Twitter for whatever you want.

In fact Twitter's tagline reads 'What are you doing?' But people are using Twitter for hundreds of other things, as a networking tool, as a notebook, as a medium for self-expression, as a playground or as a meeting room. Therefore, be open-minded and think how you can use Twitter to provide value in your daily life.

Convenience

Using Twitter can take up as much or as little time as you want it to. You can quite easily spend hours reading through swathes of Tweets from friends and strangers alike. You can make it a five minute habit over coffee before you go to work, or you can mix and match, depending on what you want to do – there are no rules, and there are no limits. Twitter is working when you're not, so, you'll always catch that Tweet now or in the future because it's all stored for you. Want to go on holiday for two weeks? No problem. Want to be permanently online with Tweets landing every two seconds? No problem. It's your account to do what you will.

Chapter three

Using Twitter to promote yourself

Succeeding with Twitter

Succeeding with Twitter is not rocket science; success can mean different things for different people. Some users simply want to be 'famous' or über popular and have as many Followers as possible, others want to have access to the best information from a carefully selected network and some just want to improve the way they communicate with friends and colleagues.

You will have to learn which things work for you and which don't, depending on what you want to achieve from Twitter. We can give you some tips and some recommendations that have worked for us or our clients, but they are not absolute truths. Twitter and the way in which people communicate online using the tool is very much in its infancy – users themselves are determining the future of the application. It's a story that is being written right now, while you are reading this book, so we encourage you to use Twitter to write your part of that story.

Humanise yourself

Twitter is a great tool for humanising people; seeing a Twitter profile helps you to better understand the person behind the Tweets, seeing the new updates everyday of one person you are following bonds Follower to the Followed.

For that purpose some celebrities have started to use Twitter in a big way. Bill Clinton, former President of the United States, when in office commented on the web: *'When I took office, only high energy physicists had ever heard of what is called the Worldwide Web.... Now even my cat has its own page'.* Now the current incumbent Barrack Obama has embraced social media and is recognised as one of the most Followed users on Twitter. In a very clever move building up to the 2008 election Obama's staff utilised Twitter as a means to humanise their candidate and helped close the gap between politicians and 'ordinary working people' by using Twitter to communicate chat rather than Democrat Party dogma... Britney Spears, Shaquille O'Neal, Richard Branson and Stephen Fry are some of the celebrities using Twitter successfully and creating a close bond with the general public.

Twitter is the great democratiser – famous or not, multi-national brand or tiny start up – we all have the same tools at our disposal. If your message is a good one, users will follow you.

Effective Tweeting

Probably the intimate details of your bowel movements and what you are intending to eat for your dinner may well be of incredible interest to your friends and possibly even some of your colleagues at work – but not to the rest of the world. Twitter is many things, but it's not Facebook. It's a public tool in which all of your posts are, well, public, and therefore you don't have the 'protection' Facebook offers by only letting friends you have approved have access to your ramblings. Therefore, be super-careful how you want your Twitter persona to be viewed and interpreted by others; whether they're your Followers or not. This doesn't mean having to always be ultra-conservative. After all Twitter is all about self-expression, but be mindful if you want to use Twitter to forward your business or consulting or freelance career, think twice before posting.

For example, to Tweet 'I'm just leaving for the office now' is valuable information for friends and colleagues, especially if you know you're going to miss your nine o'clock appointment, but not particularly interesting to others who are following you on Twitter. If your Tweets only ever communicate to a small percentage of your total Followers then all of the others are not getting any value from your updates and they will eventually stop Following you. So, 'Tweet' in a diversified way, thinking about your audience always.

Gaining and retaining Followers

It always feels good when someone is listening to what you have to say, and to have tens, or hundreds or even thousands of people following your every Tweet is fantastic. Twitter can be a great way to attract and maintain an audience; to express yourself in a different and challenging way, to market your business or simply to meet new people from around the world who you would ordinarily never meet. In order to get Followers and to *keep* those Followers, you will need to Tweet about things that are interesting. Always provide good links, relevant resources, interesting articles, intelligent comments, and cite true sources if what you're posting is not your own original work. It's about using Twitter to find out more about what interests you and passing on information because you also think it will interest your Followers. Some users have a lot of Followers simply because they are adept at sharing the best information on a subject and also because they filter the wheat from the chaff so well.

Before long, you too will have created a Twitter personality, a language and a style. You will find the subjects you feel most comfortable Tweeting about, or the ones that generate the best @replies and comments and naturally people with similar interests and personalities tend to flock together.

Some tips to get more followers:

* Always include the most relevant information about yourself – your bio, your picture and your page design should transmit the same things you are trying to communicate on your Profile Page.

❋ Talk about your Twitter account through your other sites – your own web site, your Facebook account, LinkedIn, etc.

❋ Take Twitter wherever you are in the offline world; include it on your business card, in your CV, in your presentations... Twitter is a viable way others can communicate with you; don't be afraid of displaying your Twitter user name whenever you can. Those who have no idea what you're talking about soon will, and those who are in the know will warm to the way you've embraced technology – you early adopter you!

❋ Learn from users who are posting on similar topics, or companies who do what you do – if they've got more Followers than you, Follow them and see what it is they post, how often they post and what exactly it is that they're Tweeting about.

Can you offer your Followers the same, but better?

❀ Try to be the first to Tweet on a subject or to offer your comments or opinion on a topic that is already being Tweeted about – users will Follow the leader, or even a selection of leaders.

❀ Keep a very close eye on the number of people who elect to Follow you. Who are these people? Are they the sort of people you want to be Followed by and crucially, who has Unfollowed you and try to analyse the reasons why.

❀ Rather than asking yourself 'what are you doing?' Ask yourself 'what can I Tweet about to add value?'

Following the right people

Twitter isn't all about you. Communication is two way and that means at least half of your time interacting with Twitter should be spent reading what others have to say, about you, your service or a topic that interests you. In today's ultra-complex world, in which we are all interconnected and millions of messages and new content is created every single second, we have to learn how to listen. Filtering through the 'noise' is an art form and one you will master after only a few weeks of using Twitter.

One Twitter user (RT @pattiflynn) posted, 'Facebook is people you used to know. Twitter is people you'd like to know'. That comment expresses perfectly the importance of listening to others on Twitter. The little nugget is so true it needed to be added to this book – appropriately credited as a Retweet of course!

So, spend time looking at users, follow friends of your friends, read what they post and select and Follow the most relevant ones: you can always stop listening to what they say by Unfollowing them in the future, should the quality of their posts dwindle, dry up completely or begin to go off-topic.

Don't forget about your Favourites

It's fair to say that the majority of users don't use their Favourites function much. It's the small things that count and your Favourite Tweets say lots about your personality, as well as being a great way to share information that you have appreciated. There's kudos to be had if your favourite Tweets are @you from celebrities, or industry leaders in your field responding directly to you about something you have asked them. Remember, with so little opportunity to fill your profile with personal information it's by looking at the user's frequency, followers and favourites that we begin to paint a picture of that user – and if you're assessing others this way, you can rest assured that strangers (and potential clients) are doing exactly the same to you. At worst, your Favourites can act as a fantastic depository of information that you'd be hard pushed to locate easily many months from now when you've forgotten who sent it and you're following thousands of users.

Use your time effectively

Twitter, like any application of its size is easy to get lost in. There is simply so much information on offer, which is being added to every single second, that it can be overwhelming. Here are a few pointers to bear in mind.

Optimising

Don't be afraid of Following people; if you find a user with some interesting updates Follow him or her! And start to 'talk' with the user. Read what they have to say, don't be afraid of asking a question if you need to and hopefully you are on your way to a mutually beneficial Twitter relationship. The worst things that can happen are a) you are blocked from following them or b) they don't answer your @replies or your Direct Messages or c) they don't Follow you back. Don't take it personally, we're all busy bees these days and like you, they're being picky about who they interact with. Remember that everyone is on Twitter for different reasons, if someone doesn't want to interact with you, move on.

Taking care against spammers

As always, as soon as something on the web becomes popular, i.e. has a lot of visits or users, it's not too long before the spammers come in with their guns blazing trying to trick the newbies into buying Viagra, or whatever they're trying to sell this month...(sigh). The very nature of Twitter leaves a number of paths open to spammers to connect with you directly and try to entice you with their wares. Use common sense and don't follow links or information posted by suspicious Followers. You don't have to be paranoid, or fear new Followers – on the contrary, but do use your common sense. If, for example, a spectacular girl with just one update and a newly created account is following thousands of other users but is only Followed by a handful of users and her one post consists of something like 'do you think this dress fits me well? + link' you probably don't really need to click it. Twitter does a great job patrolling for suspicious activity. Generally speaking, fraudulent accounts do well to last even a couple of hours before they're shut down but we thought you should be aware.

SEO, Social, Web 2.1
David Schoenfeld

davidsc

▶ ✓ Following – Device updates OFF

David Schoenfeld

SEO, Social, Web 2.1

Email
david.schoenfeld@coseom.com

Linkedin
linkedin.com/in/davidschoenfeld

My blog
seoconsultant.es

Thanks for following me,
visit my blog or website for
more.

RT @florianwude
STRATO: http://Tw
/timostrato y http://
/quejarse...

4 minutos ago from twhirl

RT @glenngabe If you are intere
or International SEO, check out
http://is.gd/IMRX

8:27 AM Mar 4th from twhirl

Wanted to sell something on the
still not available for us "undevel
http://twitpwr.com/793/

8:25 AM Mar 4th from twhirl

Facebook has a Marketplace no
8:15 AM Mar 4th from twhirl

Tweets that stand out
Content is king but design helps content. You can run a successful Twitter account with a standard design but personalisation will help you to differentiate; a common practice is to use the Twitter background image personalisation, displaying a different design or providing some extra information.

Time your Tweets

Schedule allowing, it's far more effective to split your Twitter activity over the day rather than trying to do everything during a concentrated single period of time. Because of the instant nature of it all, if you fire off your Tweets, along with a load of @replies, you run the risk of 'spamming' your Followers as your updates effectively block all other updates. So rather than saying at 10 o'clock each morning, 'I'll check my Twitter account and that's it for the day', far better to check on your account periodically through the working day (and into the evening if you're that way inclined).

Twitter for Online Reputation Management (ORM)

Online Reputation Management consists of analysing and researching what is being said about ourselves and/or our companies on the Internet. This discipline has gained importance lately due to:

❀ Easy-to-use publishing tools: anyone and everyone has access to hundreds of publishing tools that are available on the web – it's never been easier to express opinion through blogs, videos, pictures, web pages and podcasts. Information, whether it's correct or not can be published with a few clicks and accessible to an audience of millions.

❀ More and more (and rightly or wrongly) the Internet is used as a primary information gathering tool. A web search is now the first channel we all tend to use to find out more about people or companies. Therefore what we write about ourselves and what others write about us has tremendous importance. As that information is accessible to everyone, it has to be monitored and managed.

❀ Twitter, it is clear to see, is a great tool for creating an online personality, for keeping other users informed about you, your interests or your company, but primarily it offers others a way to contact you – be ready to reply.

❀ Usually negative comments or criticism on the web are due to a lack of information or ignorance about you or your products, or a legitimate public airing of where you are letting your clients or customers down. Through Twitter you will be able to gauge how others feel about you or your services and equally, have the tools to be able to react and answer your detractors.

Never forget that your Tweets are available to all, even non-Followers, and unless you change your account, each Tweet is permanently recorded and indexed. Never Tweet something that you will later regret.

Chapter four
Using Twitter to promote your business

Companies can no longer operate with their head in the sand when it comes to social media. Twitter is really hot at the moment; it gets column inches in the offline press like no other application and it's growing like crazy. If you run, or work for a company, you have to be where your users are. It's true that, right now, Twitter is not as big as Facebook but without doubt Twitter is experiencing incredible growth and the user base is growing every single day. Twitter users are very active online and it is exactly this profile of user that you need on board with your brand as the likelihood is that if they're using Twitter, then they are creating other content too, such as blogs, comments and picture uploads. Twitter will let you know what your users are saying about you, allow you to talk to them, to keep them informed, to get the most of any new opportunities, and to increase brand awareness. For all the effort and cost associated with creating and promoting a brand, unbeknown to you, it can be being attacked, sullied and ridiculed by thousands behind your back. You'll never stop detractors from venting their spleen about their particularly bad customer experience, but you can use Twitter to reply to their anger, interact with your customers and generally limit the damage that will be done if you shy away. Web 2.0 or the social web has opened a new communication landscape, anyone and everyone can start creating and distributing content with a few clicks to a potential audience of millions and that is going to affect your company. The companies that will come out of this communication revolution smelling of roses are those who embrace and take part in this change.

Again what we say here is our approach, this is not exact science. We have our vision and best practices, but you will have to find what works best for your objectives.

For us, the key to success in terms of promoting your business via Twitter is to focus on quality and not quantity in everything you do. Show understanding and empathy with your users and offer complete transparency. This won't guarantee that you'll be loved, but you won't be far off.

Your target

Is Twitter suitable for my company? The simple answer is yes. No matter what you sell or what service you provide, there is always a way in which Twitter can help your business either as an internal or an external tool. Twitter first and foremost is a means of communication that will help you identify and interact with both potential and existing customers.

Dipping a toe in the water

If you are new to Twitter and interested in exploring the possibilities open to your organisation, then don't jump in with both feet first. Create a test or dummy account first that avoids the use of your brand. Once you create a presence on Twitter (and all forms of social media in fact) there is no way back. You are opening a communication channel with your users, and they will use it. If you are not there to answer them or to react to their requests or concerns, then you will let them down. Would you like to go inside a shop on the high street only to find that everything is out of date, items are missing or everything is soiled? What would be your impression if on entering a shop no one is there to help you? Would you buy in that shop? The answer is a resounding no. Obviously an extreme example, but one which highlights what creating a Twitter presence really means.

Think through the implications of both opening and maintaining a presence on Twitter – setting up the account is the easy bit, the difficult bit is ensuring that it's staffed from there on in.

Remember, always, it's a conversation...

Let's face it, as business owners we are not used to conversing. We have spent years of effort and resources mastering the art of unidirectional messaging by displaying aspirational ads to a passive audience watching TV, banners to encourage click-throughs to our web site, or to newspaper readers who may or may not be interested in what we have to sell. Now things are quite different, through Twitter, the great leveller, you are on parity with your customers – they have the same power as you, the same tools as you and now they have the chance to talk to you, direct. Most companies have never talked with their customers and first contacts can be tough, because sometimes the truth hurts.

Granted the criticism you receive from customers can be damning, but look at it (no matter how vitriolic or scathing) as positive criticism. Your users have taken time out from their lives to tell you where you're going wrong. Some of their suggestions may be unrealistic, some may be incredibly easy to implement. The key is to listen, to engage and to converse.

Start listening

Your brand is what your users say about it. They have more power than ever to comment on or even define what your brand is. You don't own any one communication channel anymore; communication belongs to users and crowds and the only way to ensure that your message reaches the ears and eyes of the people you want it to is to join that conversation.

But before joining in, you need to know what people are saying. In order to participate in a conversation, you have to know what the conversation is about. Have you ever felt in a work meeting that someone is talking but it is in no way related to the subject the rest of you thought you were discussing? Did you pay much attention to those comments? No, so start listening.

As Google is, and has been, the major source responsible for driving people to your web pages, Twitter is now the source of conversations relating to you, your company and your brand. Twitter allows you to track what users are saying about you in real-time, you can follow all the comments, praise and criticisms. The question is do you want to? The Twitter search is a very valuable tool for finding out what users are saying.

Twitter for research

At the same time that we listen to our users in order to understand them and to address their specific issue, we can use the information they are providing to improve our existing products by addressing where things are going wrong.

Twitter is also a great way to ask for suggestions to improve a company's customer service or product development. It is a great tool for asking user opinion and advice, a great tool to integrate user opinions in our processes and a sure step in truly becoming a more user-centric organisation.

We are not saying that you should sit back and let your Twitter Followers take any important decisions regarding strategy or new product development, but the wants, needs and ambitions of Twitter users are a valuable sounding board. The instantaneous elements of Twitter mean that you can gather user opinions about aspects of your business where you couldn't before. With Twitter you can have pretty good data back in a jiffy.

If you are interested in asking your Followers for their opinion, then there are some great tools that allow you to run Twitter polls. PollDaddy, TwtPoll and Strawpollnow, are all tools that will allow you to post a question on your Twitter account and provide the page where users can choose the answer. Just put the names into your favourite search engine to find these sites and this will possibly be the cheapest form of market research you could hope for. Importantly you'll be getting answers from users interested in your company or your products.

Communicate with your users

Now that you have read what your customers have written about you or your company, you must analyse those comments and define your objectives based on them. For example, it might be that existing or potential customers are revealing that they have lots of doubts about how to use your product correctly or are asking questions regarding specifications. It might be that users are bemoaning your customer service or, hopefully, the comments are incredibly positive and users are recommending your products or services to others. Obviously depending on what users are saying, your approach needs to be different.

Just by registering with Twitter and starting to publicly interact with customers on a general or one-to-one basis is a huge step. It's perceived by the recipients and by observers as you seriously paying attention to your users' needs; placing users at the centre of your company, as it should have always been. Joining Twitter conversations will personalise both your company and the staffer who is actually Tweeting. You will no longer be an impersonal corporation and users will appreciate it. Remember the old adage – people like people, not brands and Twitter can be a great tool for creating a trusting relationship with your users.

Therefore as a business you can start a Twitter conversation to:

❀ Improve your customer service;
❀ Provide information;
❀ Reply to criticism;
❀ Offer customer feedback and suggestions.

Some tips:

- ❀ Be personal;
- ❀ Use your user's language;
- ❀ Be prepared for criticism;
- ❀ Remember Twitter belongs to the community. Show respect. Twitter is a place in which lots of users are having a great experience and you can't just jump in and start shouting 'Here I am! Play by my rules.'

For a master class in customer services through Twitter, check out Frank Eliason's efforts on behalf of his employer Comcast. Frank spends hours on Twitter (his Twitter handle is @comcastcares) searching for unhappy customers and he follows up on their concerns. The results have been very positive and have left previously disgruntled customers feeling looked after, and it's only had positive effects on how Comcast is perceived by online users.

Distributing your content

As Twitter grows in popularity there will be more and more eyeballs on your content, and that means more opportunities to encourage your audience to view pages of your web site. A Twitter audience is a discerning audience. Coupled with the fact that a large number of Twitter users are 'influencers' who distribute content they like among their own networks, Retweet posts and form opinions. If your message is a good one it will spread virally. For this reason Twitter should be your first port of call when you want to gain an insight into what the public thinks about you, your products or your services.

Remember that you need to create valuable content that your audience can react to, not just promotional messages which are often regarded as spam.

Gaining attention

When someone starts Following your company Twitter messages, that means he is volunteering that he is interested, for one reason or another, in your organisation. That relationship has to be nurtured and can't be abused, or Followers will leave as quickly as they came.

One really good way to ensure that your Followers feel special and privileged is to give your Followers a reward, or some form of exclusive content. If you have special offers for your Twitter Followers, or you inform users about your best promotions first via

Twitter, you will have the attention of your existing Followers as well as providing a very good reason to make people want to follow you.

Some companies and individuals, in order to get attention, start to follow Twitter users indiscriminately, without paying any attention to what that user is saying on their posts. This method of recruitment is not recommended. You need relevant users who are interested in what you have to say and you have to look for them... or let them find you. If you don't seek out the right people, or just add random users in the vain hope that because they've Tweeted about bananas they might be interested in your Smoothie bar, you will be seen as a spammer who doesn't know much about Twitter or your audience. Engage rather than bully your users with your brand or product.

Techcrunch use Twitter to offer Followers the chance to trial new products. Atrapalo, a Spanish shopping site, offers special promotions (really, really cheap flights, for example) exclusively via Twitter, a sure fire way to attract just the right kind of Follower who is interested in purchasing their products.

❀ Post exclusive and relevant information.
❀ Offer an incentive to the people who follow you; i.e. a Twitter-only promotion or an exclusive discount.
❀ Track your brand/product and reply to the people who mention it. Interact with them, providing the information they need or publicly address their concerns.
❀ Don't focus just on your product/brand, but on the wider subjects related to it. Use Twitter to locate potential users and start a conversation with them.

❀ Remember, don't hammer home the company
  message… get users to trust you first, business
  will follow for sure.

But the most important lesson from all this is not to
become obsessed with increasing your Followers,
just to get big numbers – it is better to have one
happy relevant customer than hundreds of them not
interested in you, and far more than you can possibly
converse with via Twitter.

Online Reputation Management (ORM)
We looked at the importance of ORM in Chapter 3
when we were referring to individuals. For
companies, online reputation is equally important.
Existing and potential customers will use the internet
to find out more about your products and your

company. They look for reviews and some of them even write them, they share opinions and in some cases they criticise what you're doing.

As we have mentioned already, Twitter is a great tool for research. To find out what users are saying, you can use the search functionality and look for what is being said regarding your products. This will drive you to some unsatisfied users or users that need more information. Dealing with those users, providing information, listening to them and making them feel part of the company will decrease the number of unsatisfied customers, and at the same time you will generate a trust and transparent image that others will flock to.

Whenever a person finds your company Twitter account, they should find an approachable and human brand, ready to help and one that clearly cares about their customers.

Twitter and SEO

Search Engine Optimisation (SEO) is the process of increasing traffic from search engines and due to the importance that search engines have achieved, SEO activities are without doubt critical to your online presence. Twitter as we will see affects this process:

Links and the <nofollow> tag

One of the most important things to improve your rankings in search engines are links pointing to your site ('backlinks' as they are known in SEO terminology). In a nutshell, search engines consider a link to a site like a vote of confidence, so the more links to your site, the more votes you have and therefore search engines consider your site more important.

A <nofollow> tag is an instruction to the search engines not to follow a link to its destination and to essentially ignore it. Twitter could be a great tool for generating thousands if not millions of links, because every time you post a web address in your Tweet this could be a valuable backlink to your web site. In fact lots of people are including their URLs in their Tweets for that express reason. However, what they don't realise is that Twitter is adding a <nofollow> tag to those links essentially nullifying them from an SEO perspective.

Why? Well, if links within Tweets were taken into account by search engines, spammers would immediately try to take advantage of it and flood Twitter with useless links

and spam. For that reason, Twitter is adding the
<nofollow> tag to ensure the party isn't ruined by
spammers and abuse of the system.

So should you include links to your web site or not?
Of course! Although it won't count as a backlink in
SEO terms, if there is a need to post a web address
on a Tweet to inform Followers about something,
then include it. Distribution of good content is a
good SEO strategy; good content is referred and
linked to by other users.

Tiny URLs

There is a misunderstanding that converting a URL
into a Tiny URL means that it is useless in SEO terms.
Actually that is not the case. You see Tiny URLs use
what is called a '301 redirect', which means that the

site has been moved permanently to another address, which is in fact the real URL.

Without getting too technical, the important thing you should know is that '301 redirects' are the right way to keep 'SEO power' or 'linking juice' from one URL to another.

Tiny URLs are effective in your SEO strategy; it is Twitter's addition of the <nofollow> tag that means they don't count as a backlink on Twitter.

A link… is always a link

Although links posted within Tweets are not relevant for search engines, don't forget that you are able to add a link within your profile to your web site. The web page you point to on your profile does not have a <nofollow> tag so it will indeed assist with your search engine's rankings.

Detecting trends

In SEO he who shouts first, shouts loudest and anticipating your audience is key.

Twitter is a great way to visualise trends and observe hot topics. SEO at the end of the day is related to keywords and Twitter is a great tool to track those keywords in real-time conversations. Yes, you might not be able to harness the full might of backlinks, but backlinks are only a small part of search engine optimisation and not the be all and end all of a successful SEO strategy.

So, instead you can focus your attention on Twitter to see what is becoming interesting, which keywords users are using in order to create relevant articles or content. Therefore Twitter is a great way to both anticipate and to monitor interesting subjects, and to ensure that you are first to know what is already or is becoming important.

Some tools like Tweetscoop offer what are called Tag Clouds, which are visual depictions of site content. The most popular words look bigger and the less popular ones are smaller. We are sure you have seen several of them but just in case you haven't, they look like this:

This simple visualisation technique can really help you to spot trends.

Buzzing right now

afford   alright   alternative american   believes b
   cigarette   courtney curious   dang def
guardian   hat haters   hood   hugh idol   jan
   letter level   longest lou   mcdonalds mich

mountains moves neighbors pept

   plate politics pope positive prepping   re
sean   security shares shower soccer   soo

      sushi sydney tim   w2e weight w

01:36:10

calm   capture   chocolate
gah   gaming   grill
y   judge kevin   keynote
id   midnight   mitchel

nds   piece

eilly rose   routine   salt
stimulus   success survey

redwedto

Appearing in the search results

Twitter posts and accounts appear on Search Engine Result Pages (SERPs), especially if you have linked to them from other sites (such as your blog or your web site).

Using Twitter regularly and including relevant keywords in your Tweets will increase your Twitter account visibility on search results, whether or not the search engine user is a Twitter user. This is a great way to drive that traffic to your web site.

Real-time search

Everyday Twitter is being used to perform searches and in that sense it becomes another player in the search arena where we should try to display our pages.

Some people prefer the real-time information offered by Twitter than the older results offered by Google or Yahoo! In examples such as sporting events or breaking news, real-time information is the most highly valued and Twitter Tweets get a great position.

Social search

Twitter has a human touch that none of the major search engines have. In Google, Yahoo! or MSN Live Search, results are built by an algorithm, basically by a machine. Conversely, Twitter results are created by humans so, to find out who sells a certain book, you can go and look for it on Google, but you can look for it on Twitter to see if anyone has an opinion about it, and if there hasn't been an opinion offered, you could ask for one.

Recommendations from friends or fellow Twitter users are more valuable than the marketing blurb provided by those trying to sell a product, and it's providing that human factor that Twitter does so well.

Geo-located searches

One of the areas with great potential in terms of SEO is geo-located searching, just as we will give more weight to things that our actual Followers say, or those who we are Following are saying. Often the information that is being created near us is of more relevance (to our lives, to our market) than what's happening in other countries or even cities.

Twitter has the potential to determine geographic location of Tweets and users, based on the information offered in the profile pages and also because of the high participation of mobile users. Although currently this information isn't being utilised, it could easily become an important part of Twitter's future and will only help those of us with businesses to promote through Twitter by allowing greater access to targeted segments of Twitter users. It's not hard to imagine Twitter accounts that are city or even town specific rather than countrywide and the potential is huge.

Twitter and web metrics

What impact is Twitter having on your site? Which subjects interest your Twitter audience the most? Use your web analytics system to know your Twitter audience and the quantity of traffic Twitter is driving to your site. All web analytics systems have a 'referrals' section which are sites that drive visits to your site; Twitter will be one of these referrers. Try to correlate visits and Tweets in order to know which of them are the most successful. For example, if one day you were Tweeting about a specific subject and you see an increase in visits coming from Twitter, this means that that subject is particularly interesting to your Twitter audience, and hopefully they will be referring to your posts, or Retweeting them around the Twittersphere. Twitter users are early adopters and influencers, therefore, if you get them excited about something, you can be sure that they'll pass on the message to the masses.

Twitpwr (http://twitpwr.com) deserves a special mention. This tool is primarily a URL shortening service, but it provides you with information about how many times your links have been clicked, which we think is really valuable information.

Dealing with identity

❀ Shall I use a corporate Twitter account, with the name of my company and my logo?

❦ Wouldn't it be better to personalise my brand, putting real faces to the company?

❦ Should I encourage Twitter usage between my employees?

Actually we are not able to give you the answers to these questions, as your relationship between your business and Twitter must be defined by you. Probably the best thing, initially, is to do a little bit of everything until you find your feet with Twitter and you can measure what sort of impact your activity is having.

Having a purely corporate Twitter presence is a good way to create an official channel of communication as it is centralised and easy to control, but you miss some 'personalisation'.

On the other hand, if you start a Twitter account as a brand representative, other Twitter users appreciate the human touch and the intimacy. Company CEOs often create Twitter accounts as it is a great way of achieving direct communication with customers in a personal way.

We're big believers in encouraging your employees to Tweet; to become the face and the communal voice of your company to the Twitter world. It can be really powerful, gets you even more mentions and eyeballs, but of course comes with risk – as an over-enthusiastic employee (or worse, a disgruntled employee) can post whatever they like unless everything is monitored – but don't let this stop you. The social web is here which means you no longer control communication about your brand anymore.

Embrace this change and let your employees engage with existing and potential customers.

Whatever you decide to do, be sure you are being honest and transparent, if you are caught creating fake profiles or posting false information about your own products or your competitors, you will receive an impressive backlash from the community.

A mainline to your customers

Twitter offers you access to your existing and potential customers in a way that email can't. You might have thousands of customers who have opted-in to receive email notifications and you can have a world-beating customer relationship management system (CRM) to ensure that you are sending the most targeted email to the correct segment of your customer base – but despite this, your email may not be read, or the links not clicked, or it might end up in a spam folder... But not with Twitter. If they're Following you, that Tweet will be served and if it's of interest then customers will act.

Don't confuse customers

Although we've stressed the importance of using your Twitter account to show your company as approachable, friendly and 'down with new technology', the appearance of your Twitter page/s and the tone of your Tweets must still reinforce your brand messages and the house-style being used across your other marketing channels. Obviously using the same logo or device and corporate colours is a good idea and although the style of your Tweets can be more casual, that doesn't mean that grammar and spelling go out the window. Yes, it's fine to abbreviate and use 'Twitter language' but it must be clear at all times that this is the official Twitter account of your company. The member of staff responsible for updating the account has to understand both the direction and message of the company as well as what Twitter is, and what it isn't.

Promoting your presence on Twitter

We're quickly running out of space on our business cards, but just as you'd include your web address on your card or on your email signature block, it's now time to include your Twitter user name. Likewise, if you've got your Twitter account up and running, make sure that there's a link on your web site offering users the chance to 'Follow You'.

Brand monitoring

In today's social web or Web 2.0 scenario you need to know exactly what people are saying about you, in real-time, in order to stop bad reviews or criticism spreading and causing incalculable damage. Likewise, if there are other users or companies singing your praises, you'll want to take advantage of positive comments, reviews and goodwill. In order to know what people are saying about your brand/product, Twitter is the perfect tool. You can track what users are saying in real-time and use Twitter search to be able to see all references to your brand, with the latest displayed first. Later in the book we will have a look at more advanced applications based on Twitter tools like Splitweet, which gives you some extra features such as the ability to track brand or product mentions.

What about your team?

We have been talking about Twitter for conversing with your customers, but what about internal communications? You could use Twitter for creating a new communication channel between people on your team, especially effective if your team includes home workers or team members in different geographical locations. Twitter can therefore act as a way to bring team members together and keep them up to date, and at the same time add to the information available about your company, all the time allowing other Twitter users the opportunity to partake in discussions.

Remember that your updates are accessible to everyone, so there are obviously some occasions were internal email is better.

Twitter in times of crisis

Fast, overtly public and easy-to-access information makes Twitter great for crisis communications. A common criticism in times of crisis is the lack of fast, accurate and up to the minute information, and this is exactly what Twitter offers. The perfect way to provide the latest information to a huge potential audience.

Imagine your servers are down and your web site is not accessible; you have hundreds or thousands of users who don't know what is going on… imagine some of those users are Twitter users and on receiving an error message when trying to access your web site they look for you through Twitter search. Through Twitter they can read 'Our servers are down, we are working as fast as possible to fix them' and you are able to keep updating that information: 'We fixed the problem in less than an hour, we should be back on the air in about 20 minutes', showing clearly how the status is changing. This is definitely going to help your users and you will be regarded as a company that knows how to deal with problems.

Taking the same premise even further, if it were your web server that was down, you could continue to post news, information, reviews or whatever through your Twitter account. Customers would be relieved to learn that 'The problem is just affecting our web site, the rest of our operations are continuing as usual', allowing you to limit the damage and manage customer expectations.

Zappos as an example of how to use Twitter effectively

Zappos is an online shoe retailer in the US and its use of Twitter is a good example of how this new communication tool can help your business strategy.

Twitter usage has spread throughout the organisation from the top down. Toni Hsieh, the Zappos CEO, has an account and it is the most visible part of the company. He uses his Twitter account to tell Followers what he is up to as well as communicating the corporate message and vision.

Toni is the most popular Zappos Twitter user, but all employees are encouraged to participate in Twitter, in fact they get training in how to use Twitter effectively. The result is that there are hundreds of

Zappos employees on Twitter, and each of them is able to solve problems, put a human face to the company and show users how Zappos works and how cool they all are! Zappos doesn't look like a corporate machine, but instead a personable and approachable company that listens to its customers. Twitter is helping them to build an honest and close relationship with customers which no other medium could do.

On top of that Zappos displays all Tweets that include the keyword Zappos on their web site (good and bad) – this incredible level of transparency tells existing and potential customers, 'we care about what users say about us and we are not afraid of it'. It's not hard to see why Zappos sales have increased dramatically over the last 12 months.

Chapter five
Twitter clients and applications

Twitter application development

Twitter is most often accessed through its web site (www.twitter.com) and accessed via your browser (Safari, Firefox, Internet Explorer...) but Twitter has numerous desktop and mobile clients that extend many of the Twitter functionalities, like Tweeting in different accounts or being notified when someone has stopped Following you. On Twitter's own blog (http://blog.twitter.com) it is written, *Twitter has a warm spot for innovative simplicity and an open approach to technology development. We make use of open source software when it makes sense and we think it brings good karma to contribute back to the open source community whenever possible.* This apparently socialist ideology may seem incredibly philanthropic but it's a great model – allow other individual companies or developers to interact with your product and you get more and more people interacting with Twitter in ways even the founders didn't previously think of – which makes Twitter one of the fastest growing fields of application development.

Twitter for mobiles

But if Twitter fits a platform perfectly, then it's not the web but in fact the mobile phone where Twitter truly excels. Twitter's easy-to-use functionality, plus its immediacy makes it perfect for mobiles. Twitter is perfect for those short moments that we have over the day; waiting for a bus or train, or waiting for your rice to boil... Tweeting takes the same time it takes to send an SMS (remember the 140 character rule) and there are still times when it's simply easier to access a mobile phone than a computer. Do remember that enabling your mobile will mean a surge or possibly hundreds of SMSs hitting your phone inbox – this can be overwhelming but managed properly mobile Tweeting is a really exciting function.

URL shorteners

One thing you'll notice quite quickly when looking at users' posts on Twitter is the propensity to use links. Why? Well this is the quickest way to point people to the information you want them to read, to a web site where there are no character limits. Now what you may have also noticed is that the URLs aren't the usual huge wrapped links we've got used to on blogs or contained within the body of an email – instead they seem to be quite small. The 140 character rule is changing how we utilise space. Include an enormous URL in your Tweet and there won't be much room left for anything else (if you're trying to include a URL which includes tracking codes and points to a specific article from a large web site, chances are that the URL will be over 140 characters!). So what's a girl to do?

URL shorteners are the answer. These services allow you to enter a target URL of any length and with the click of your mouse it is altered into a shorter (around 20 characters) URL which leaves you enough characters to explain why the link is worthwhile visiting and of course what people will find there. But what about tracking how many people click through? Well, the good news is that you can still track through the host site that shortened the URL for you. Net result, you have a user-friendly URL you can use, with all the bells and whistles you would have had with the original one.

And the best bit? They're free! Check out the following sites:

http://tinyurl.com

http://bit.ly

http://twitturly.com

Using Twitter smarter...employing clients

These aren't your business contacts or your customers. We're talking about software applications that allow you quicker access to Twitter on the move or from the comfort of your armchair. Basically, a Twitter client is the platform that allows you to perform the basic Twitter actions; sending updates, seeing your received Tweets and your Direct Messages without having to log on to Twitter.com. Using that broad definition, hundreds of applications are in effect, clients. In order to make things a little bit easier we've classified them as phone clients, browser clients or desktop clients.

Please note that this isn't a definitive list, just our personal favourites and as with all web-based technology there's always something new just around the corner.... so keep your eyes peeled!

Ring Ring...phone clients

Twitter has caught the imagination of so many, so quickly, because it facilitates real-time 'conversation'. Its sheer simplicity, ease of use and basic rules make it perfect for use via mobile phone. It wasn't so long ago that on seeing my first mobile phone, my mother commented, 'Only doctors and drug dealers need mobile phones, and I know you're not a doctor... ' Now the world and his friend has one (even my mother). It was no accident that the character limit for Twitter was set with the same limitation as SMS and thus, some of the first clients built for Twitter were with the mobile user in mind. This particular part of Twitter's development was sheer genius. Social marketing shouldn't just be limited to the web – and with Twitter it's not. Everyone has a phone and everyone is online, so let's make sure our product works across both platforms. It's so clever I want to cry...

Of course, the huge range of mobile phones out there all produced by different manufacturers does mean you'll have to look around for a client that fits both your needs and complies with your phone, but whatever device you're using (BlackBerry, iPhone, Android, SmartPhone, etc.) you should be able to find a compatible client.

Ring Ring (but soooo much sexier)... the iPhone
Twitterrific is currently the most popular phone-based Twitter client. There is a free, ad-supported version and a paid for, ad-free version. This client has a great interface and is quite easy to use, especially effective for reading and tracking @replies and Direct Messages.

iTweet is a great interface and gaining quickly in popularity. This client adds another dimension by offering a URL shortener, threaded conversations when you have received an 'in reply to' and a TwitPic uploader.

PocketTweet is another jazzy interface that looks good on the iPhone and features all of the basic Twitter functionality.

There are more, and there will be more clients released; if you're an iPhone user you'll be well supported as the ease of use of the iPhone makes it the perfect mobile host to carry Twitter.

Desktop clients

Maybe you don't particularly like having to visit www.twitter.com every time you want to post a

Tweet or read the Tweets of others. Well, the great news is that you don't have to. A number of desktop applications have been developed which can run on your computer while you get on with whatever else you want to; every time there's an update you are notified. There's a bunch of good desktop applications available including:

Tweetdeck. One of the best clients in terms of how information is displayed. Spend about ten seconds setting up your three column layout and you're ready to go – general Tweets will fall into one column, @replies into another and Direct Messages into a third. This is Twitter made easy. Where it really comes into its own is when it's applied as a 'Twitter Screen', something utilised at events, conferences and shows. You can, for example, display your Twitter account via your Tweetdeck on a large display screen. This can be observed by your offline audience and can be operating in the background so any new Tweets offering questions or comments will appear on the Tweetdeck in real-time – visible to the speaker and the audience. A great way to amplify a conversation and a really interesting way to run a Q&A session.

Twhirl. Very similar to the Tweetdeck in functionality, its appearance is more 'classic Twitter'. It does however offer the ability to manage multiple accounts through a single control panel.

Spaz. An open source desktop client for Mac, Windows and Linux and allows a high degree of personalisation features. Looks great and it's nice to have running in the background while you get on with doing other stuff (for example, I'm writing this book!).

Browser clients

Why would I go to another browser client when I can just use www.twitter.com? Well, browser clients offer you different or extended functionality depending on their theme. Desktop apps are great, but they're limited to one user – the user of the PC or Mac it's installed on. The great thing about Browser clients is that they're on the web, which means anyone in your company with the correct account details can log on. This allows you to have multiple users across the globe 24/7, should you wish.

Splitweet. Very interesting for marketers as it allows you to Tweet with different accounts. Companies, as they get more into digital marketing and start developing more complex and difficult to manage accounts and content need something a bit more specific than the Twitter web site. Splitweet can help you to manage all your accounts from one place. It also focuses heavily on the Twitter search which makes it really easy to find any @replies, Tweets or mentions of you, your brand or your products. Let Splitweet know what you want to track and it will do the hard work.

Twitterbar. A Firefox extension that sits like a toolbar at the top of your FireFox browser and allows you to post a Tweet from your address bar. It only allows you to post, so using it, you can make the mistake of constantly Tweeting without taking the time to read what others are Tweeting about.

PowerTwitter. A relatively new face to the web-client market, PowerTwitter is a Firefox add on that makes Twitter more like Facebook – the ability to play video and music, share photos with greater ease as well as tracking tools – it's a 'single glance' viewer that's set to become über-popular. Check it out.

Twitter Gadget for iGoogle. If you use iGoogle's personalised Google start page, then this Twitter gadget will allow you to see your 'Following' Tweets and post direct to Twitter.

Twitter Netvibes Widget. If you are a Netvibes user, you can integrate the Twitter widget so you can see any updates in your personalised page.

There are more, many more out there. And there will be even more next week. You will no doubt download a few, play with them for a while and either uninstall or continue using. The important thing is all of these applications allow you to perform the basic Twitter functions but also choose to expand one or more functionalities to make your life easier. You'll find the tool that suits you and your needs best. And if you do find a new app that rocks your world, we'd love to know about it! Send us a Tweet @sanseng or @josellinares and you'll get a mention in future books.

Twitter for the serious business user...

At time of writing it's still in private beta, but a really exciting development is CoTweet which is a comprehensive business platform that will empower companies to do many of the things suggested in this book through one single interface. If you're already using Twitter to any degree commercially and you're prepared to take part in their regular feedback meetings, then you too can apply to join the private beta.

Chapter six
Twitter on steroids: extending the uses of Twitter

So we have explored several interesting ways to apply Twitter to promote yourself and your brand. Despite Twitter being an incredibly simple concept, it's that sheer simplicity that gives you myriad possibilities. But what's next?

Just the start

Twitter designers and developers set out with the right philosophy – create a simple service that is open to everyone and allows others to expand its usage and engage with Twitter any way they see fit.

A great decision from the start was to make Twitter updates compatible with RSS, a standardised data format that makes it really easy to share and manipulate the information across myriad platforms. This ensured that content could transcend the medium of Twitter.com (which was already web and mobile friendly) and be seamlessly integrated with other blogs and syndicated content web sites.

But this of course wasn't enough, so Twitter opened the door to outside developers expanding the uses and usage of Twitter further by including an open API (Application Programming Interface), which basically means that with a bit of technical knowledge you or your technical team can access Twitter's internal functionalities and exploit it. It's easier to explain with a few real-world examples.

One of the basic Twitter functionalities is updating your status in less than 140 characters. Twitter open API lets you do it without needing to go to Twitter.com. With some programming skills you could create an application that would allow you to update your status from your desktop, through a browser application or via your mobile phone.

You could also build an application which would monitor your new Followers. Who is following you today, who is no longer following you and even include some sort of reporting or statistical analysis such as their location. All of this information is of course available through Twitter.com, but you'd have to look at each account page separately. A tool could do it for you automatically, 24 hours a day, seven days a week.

Experimenting with the Twitter API does require some programming skills, but don't worry if you don't have them. As you've seen there's literally hundreds of applications being built to interact with Twitter, and if you've spotted a gap in the market, then you'll now know how to explain what you require from a developer and be able to justify why it would be a good idea to build. It's highly likely that if you need an application for your business, then so do other people – you could monetise whatever you build in-house by selling it on to others.

Analysis and statistics

If your purpose is to have as many eyeballs as possible Following you and reading your Tweets then the good news is that there are a whole host of quantitative data based tools that can help you. There are tools to help you search, tools to monitor the success of your Tweets and tools to track new Followers and users who have Unfollowed you which can all be displayed as easy-to-read graphs and tables. Here are some of them:

Twitterholic gives you a detailed view of your total activity on Twitter. Great for creating reports and to prove how successful you were (or not) using Twitter.

Tweetstats will show you advanced graphs regarding your Twitter usage (users who you replied to the most, your updating frequency and much more).

Qwitter will inform you when someone has stopped Following you, a great tool to find out what interests your audience and possibly an insight into what doesn't!

133

Research

There is also a whole host of tools for gathering information to help you to understand your audience and your market better:

Tweetbeep is a basic alert system where you will be notified every time your targeted keywords are Tweeted on the Twittersphere.

Twitscoop allows you to detect trends and activity of certain keywords. The results are displayed as graphs which makes it very easy to understand and great for including in reports. It is really interesting to see how popular a keyword becomes when a new service is launched (i.e. Google Chrome) or when a service fails or the latest blockbuster film is released.

Retweetist keeps you informed about which Tweets are the most referenced, i.e. the most Retweeted.

Twitterbuzz lets you know which links are being Tweeted the most. As with Retweetist these are great tools just to monitor trends, but they're super cool if it's your own Tweet that you are monitoring.

Networking and community building

Building a large and effective network or community requires time, dedication and effort – here are some tools to take the donkey work out of managing a wide variety of contacts:

Mr Tweet gets recommendations about people to Follow based on having similar interests.

Twitter local gives you the opportunity to filter Tweets by location, perfect for local business!

Tweetwheel informs you which of the people you Follow know each other, very interesting networking information.

Content distribution

Creating content is all very well, but what's essential is distributing that content to the widest possible audience. Here is a tool that can really help:

Twitterfeed updates Twitter via RSS. This tool is great if you tend to update your site content shared via RSS format (blogs are the classic example). If you've got a content-rich web site already, think of the number of interesting posts that would make when delivered in distinct 140 character Tweets? Think which activities take place on your site either from your own staff writers or product managers, or the RSS feeds that you receive on the site from others. Would they be of interest to your Twitter Followers? Of course they would. If you don't already accept or receive content via RSS on your web site maybe now is the time to do so. This way when you are updating your site or your blog you'll be able to kill two birds with one stone and update your Twitter account simultaneously by updating via Twitterfeed. For example, every time you publish new industry or product news, every time new information is added to your catalogue, or every time you sign up a new business partner. For this reason Twitterfeed is one of the most powerful and interesting Twitter-based applications.

Content distribution by RSS and Twitterfeed can be used in interesting ways, such as www.conciertosbarcelona.es, a site focused on live music in Barcelona. They ensure that information about all the concerts taking place in Barcelona is published in RSS format and every day its Twitter account @conciertosbarcelona is updated with the live events going on in the city, which makes Twitter a kind of reminder service for the people who follow this account.

Twitter updaters for your blog

If you're a keen blogger then you can select an option within your blog back office to automatically post your blog updates via Twitter. This instantly lets your Twitter audience know that there's a new blog entry to read – your Tweet will include the title of the article and include a link to the entry.

MyTwitter. In contrast to the above, MyTwitter is a blog plug-in that allows you to display your Twitter updates in your blog. (We are sure you will have seen that in action on several blogs already!)

AddThis. A blog plug-in that allows users reading your blog to Tweet a link to your blog post.

What's clear is that a lot of blogs are feeding Twitter accounts and vice versa. The fact that lots of bloggers and the blog sites themselves are incorporating shared plug ins to social networks and nearly all of them allow you to share content on Twitter, gives you some idea about how important Twitter is becoming for content and information distribution.

Twitter for photography

Twitter, rightly or wrongly is limited to 140 characters of text, but don't worry, some organisations understand the importance of photography and have developed ways to incorporate pictures with Twitter. There are a number of services that allow you to upload a photo to a web page and then include a link to that photo on your Tweet.

Twitpic. The most popular service (at the moment) for adding links to your photos on your Tweets.

Focus on the important part...

It's likely that you feel a bit overwhelmed right now with the plethora of applications, widgets and devices relating to Twitter. All those applications and uses...there simply aren't enough hours in the day. The reality is Twitter is still in early-phase development and new applications are being created nearly every day. At the time of writing there's stuff in development that will allow you to synchronise Twitter with Apple iCal, to be used as a reminder tool, to keep track of your costs, to keep track of your smoking habits, customer services for enterprises... Twitter-based applications are becoming complex and you will need to keep abreast of what's hot and what's not. Exploring is fun, and for the one hundred applications that you try that don't quite cut the mustard, rest assured you'll find one gem that makes your life easier and offers you new opportunities with Twitter that were simply not possible last month. Likewise, if you see a need for an application that doesn't exist, build it (or have it built) and you could be a pioneer.

It's an exciting time in terms of how communication and the distribution of information is changing. But the best is yet to come. In the words of Amazon's founder and CEO Jeff Bezos, 'It's still only day one'.

See you in the corporate Twittersphere.

Chapter seven
Twitter in the future,
Twitter fiction

A threat to Google?

We don't know what the state of play will be when you read this, but right now some people see Twitter as a threat to Google, probably the only one. We think there could be great synergy between the services rather than one being a threat to the other. There are also rumours within the Twittersphere and within other internet communities that predict Google will offer to buy Twitter (no doubt for a very healthy fee) to protect themselves and also to quickly monetise the real-time search results with a form of AdSense and AdWords. Watch this space...

We have mentioned that Twitter is real-time, allowing for real-time conversation and therefore real-time search. Life nowadays goes fast, faster than ever before. Because information goes out of date in days, even in hours, Twitter provides a very valuable service that leaves email and search engines lagging behind. We don't see Google search being replaced by Twitter, but Twitter will take at least a portion of Google search traffic, as this new kind of real-time searching is valuable. As the web continues to evolve, the information itself will become more important than the web site that actually carries it.

Twitter has another thing that Google doesn't have and that is the human touch. When you conduct a search on Google you are asking a computer programme what is the most relevant site for a specific set of keywords. With Twitter you can ask real people the same question. Instead of going to Google search to ask for 'cinema movie weekend' you can go to Twitter users and ask 'Can you recommend a film showing this weekend?' As you can see, the whole concept is different.

Twitter includes a human factor in searches. Instead of looking for a web site, now you can ask your followers a question and get an answer or opinion and/or a web site recommendation. With Google you only get a web site recommendation. OK, right now this is quite limited, but imagine what the scene will be like if Twitter achieves 20 million users, or 100 million? This collective consciousness is a very exciting prospect indeed.

Everyone in the world talking to each other!

The Internet was a revolution because it allowed information to be accessed by absolutely anyone with an Internet connection, wherever they were. After over a decade and a half of using the Internet, our information consuming habits have changed dramatically. Today, both studying and working practices are completely different things and now the Internet is changing the way that we socialise.

Twitter can become the tool that will allow the world to talk to each other, a new kind of human communication that is global. Chaotic it might be at the moment, but it's radically new, so new that it is difficult to measure its future impact on culture.

A new page of history. Twitter as the mankind diary

When we study history we focus on the big events, Christopher Columbus and America, Napoleon and Waterloo, Hannibal and the Alps. It seems that history is a snapshot of great people and great deeds. What history tends to gloss over is the countless generations of humans whose contributions were small and yet make up the 99.99% of history that ensure that our world works the way it does today but whose stories didn't make it into the history books or even Wikipedia. That combined knowledge along with those hopes, aspirations and opinions have been erased from history.

Web 2.0 and specifically Twitter, assuming that all Tweets are preserved, will allow others in the future to get an accurate picture of life today, our daily lives effectively acting as a mankind diary; a diary where our descendants will see 'what we were doing, in 140 characters or less'.

In conclusion

We have been talking about Twitter as a new communication tool, as both a destination and a tool to converse and to share information; Twitter as a solution for these fast moving times. But what next? If it really is only day one then we are at the beginning. Maybe in two years no one will be talking about or using Twitter anymore or maybe in two years Twitter will have truly revolutionised the way in which we communicate. We have hopefully succeeded in showing you examples of how Twitter can work for you or your business now, but nothing is ever exhaustive and new ways to apply Twitter will come and go. So, be aware that these are indeed interesting times; a social media revolution is taking place and as with all revolutions, you can be an onlooker or a participant; your contribution may not be huge, but those small ideas are the ones that make the difference. Join the conversation and create your own part of history out there.

Good luck and happy Tweeting.

Index